THE SCHOOL
THAT BUILT A TOWN

by Walter Hines Page

With an Introductory Chapter

by Roy E. Larsen
*Chairman, National Citizens Commission
for the Public Schools*

HARPER & BROTHERS, PUBLISHERS, NEW YORK

To the Honored Memory of
My Father
whose work was work that
built up the commonwealth

Preface

OLD JEFF MEDDLIN LIVED IN A RAMSHACKLE HOUSE,
ploughed a poor farm, made a cross-mark for his signa-
ture, led prayers in the congregation, and only twice in
his life went out of the county where he was born. He
was a man with a strong body and with good sense; but
his thought travelled in narrow ways, and dyspepsia
wore him out before he grew old. Young Jeff is very like
his father, with this difference, that he indulges in drink
instead of prayer; and Jeff 3d, a lad of good parts, has
started life on the level where old Jeff died. The family
for three generations has not got out of its shirt-sleeves.

Their neighbour, Colonel Graham, says, "Some men
will rise and some men will not. Nothing can lift up the
Meddlins." With this comfortable irresponsibility, he has
never seriously thought of their potential value to the
State, nor (since they have always voted for him) as
sovereign and possibly dangerous citizens. He sees men
ranged in clearly defined classes, but he has never
thought of them as a democracy. Nor has he ever in-
cluded his thriftless black neighbour, Sam Goode, in his
thoughts of citizenship except at election times, when

Sam, though dependent on him, has always voted against him.

Now, when I think of the community where Colonel Graham lives and of its future, I think not only of him but of the Meddlins and of the Goodes as well; and I have on several occasions, by tongue and by pen, tried to convince him that the very virtue of a democracy is that by the right training of all its children it has the power constantly to reinforce itself from the rear.

What I have written and said to him makes up this little book. If I have repeated many things many times (things, too, that were old before I was born), it is fair to ask the reader to remember that Colonel Graham is somewhat deaf and hard to convince. I will thank the reader to remember, too (as an old English writer reminded the prince whose patronage he sought), that "the Author's worst Publick Crime is that he is an Ill Writer."

W. H. P.

May, 1902

Contents

The Fight For Better Schools

1826-1952

BY ROY E. LARSEN

> *I believe in the free public training of both the hands and the mind of every child born of woman.*
>
> *I believe that by the right training of men we add to the wealth of the world. All wealth is the creation of man, and he creates it only in proportion to the trained uses of the community; and, the more men we train, the more wealth everyone may create.*
>
> *I believe in the perpetual regeneration of society, in the immortality of democracy, and in growth everlasting.*
>
> —WALTER HINES PAGE

IN THESE WORDS WALTER HINES PAGE, WITH ALL THE literary talent that made him a great man, summed up his whole philosophy of American education half a century ago. They are as true and pertinent today as they were when he delivered them at the commencement of the State Normal School at Athens, Georgia, on December 11, 1901. His credo of American education was his deep conviction that the only acceptable measure of any civilization was the extent to which it improved the condition of the common citizen. It shines brightly through this volume of three essays making the case for the public school system fifty years ago—and through his whole career as scholar, editor, journalist, publisher and ambassador to the Court of St. James's during the First World War.

Walter Hines Page knew from personal experience whereof he spoke. He was born in North Carolina just before the Civil War. He grew up against the backdrop of Reconstruction. The public school system of his state seemed shattered beyond repair or recovery. The old prejudices against broad popular education were still strong in the postwar South. As Burton Hendricks puts it in his *Life and Letters of Walter H. Page*:

> In any real sense there was no publicly supported system for training the child. A few wretched hovels, scattered through a sparsely settled country, served as school houses; a few uninspired and neglected women, earning perhaps $50 or $75 a year did weary duty as teachers; a few groups of anemic and listless children, attending school for only forty days a year—such was the preparation for life which most Southern states gave the less fortunate of their citizens. The glaring fact that emphasized the outcome of this official carelessness was an illiteracy, among white men and women, of 26 per cent. Among the Negroes it was vastly larger.

Born into such an unfavorable educational environment, young Page managed to survive its evil influences

by his own talents, and his parents' determination to give
him the best possible education. At the age of twenty-
one he was selected to be one of the first twenty Fellows
at the new Johns Hopkins University at Baltimore. There
for two years he responded to the admonition of Johns
Hopkins' founding president, Daniel Coit Gilman:
"Gentlemen, you must light your own torch."

Throughout the rest of his life Walter Page engaged
himself in helping to light the torch for succeeding generations of Southern children.

Although his career took him north of the Mason-
Dixon line for long periods, his influence on the development of education in the South was continuous and
effective. Throughout his life, through his personal letters, his published articles, and frequent visits and
speeches in the South, he worked for the schools of his
native state and region.

Because Mr. Page was one of those rare citizens of an
earlier age who recognized children as the nation's greatest resource, his words have a timeless relevance to
American education and its problems. Except for his
statistics, he could be talking directly to the thousands
and thousands of citizens throughout this land who are
organized into community groups to defend, maintain
and improve the local public school systems. They share
the same inspiration in behalf of this American institution, the same sense of honorable endeavor to preserve

and develop in a never-ending continuity the very foundation of their nation's democracy.

Some months ago Professor Henry Steele Commager, historian and author, surveyed the accomplishments of the schools of America and concluded that "No other people ever demanded so much of education as have the American; none other was ever served so well by its schools and its educators.

"From the beginning," he wrote, "education has had very special and very heavy tasks to perform. Democracy could not work without an enlightened electorate, and education has been required to provide the enlightenment. The various states, regions and sections that made up the nation could not achieve unity without a sentiment of nationalism, and education was expected to inculcate that sentiment. The nation could not absorb millions and tens of millions of immigrants from all parts of the globe without some method of rapid and effective Americanization, and the schools were called on to be the chief agencies of this process. Economic and social distinctions, privilege, and class consciousness threatened to corrode and destroy democracy itself and upon schools fell a large part of the responsibility for equalizing opportunity, and wiping out class distinctions."

All of these things our schools have done for us, and

done well. They could not have accomplished so much without the crusading aid of responsible citizens.

In 1826, for example, a citizen of Boston, William Holbrook, concerned about the fate of the new system of common schools, rallied his friends and neighbors in a campaign to preserve and develop the infant public school system. At that time the states did little or nothing to promote public education. Each community provided the quality and quantity of education it felt necessary or desirable. All too often there was little or no understanding of the value of the public school. Mr. Holbrook proposed that each community organize a lyceum with the twofold purpose of "improvement of its members in useful knowledge, and the advancement of popular education . . ." Within three years local lyceums had been formed in nearly every one of the 24 states of the Union. In 1831 a national organization, the American Lyceum, convened in its first annual meeting, and by 1832 it was reported that there were, in addition to numerous state and county lyceums, nine hundred such institutions throughout the United States.

By 1839 the work of the lyceums in arousing the interest of citizens in the common schools had been largely finished: in many instances state boards had been established to supervise the effort of the individual communities and throughout the country there was an awareness of the importance of the public school. The national organization was disbanded, but many of the local groups continued to function as centers of adult education and provided a platform for distinguished speakers of the earlier part of the nineteenth century—Henry Ward Beecher, Wendell Phillips, Oliver Wendell Holmes, Lucy Stone, Mark Twain, Ralph Waldo Emerson, Henry Thoreau and others of like stature.

One dedicated worker for the public schools who appeared often on the lyceum platform throughout New England was Horace Mann. Mann's early experience in education was destined to be influential in determining his later attitude toward public schools. What little education he had acquired in his early years he had dug for himself out of books in the Franklin, Massachusetts, Library, founded by Benjamin Franklin. Later, at the urging of a private schoolmaster, he learned enough Greek and Latin in six months to be admitted to the sophomore class at Brown University. A splendid law school record followed and in 1827, when he was twenty-one years old, he entered the Massachusetts Legislature.

His private law practice flourished; his fame as an orator spread throughout the states; his future career in politics seemed assured. By 1837 he was already president of the Massachusetts State Senate. In that year, he resigned all of his political prospects to accept the lowly post of secretary to the newly created State Board of Education. "The bar is no longer my forum," said Horace Mann. "I have abandoned jurisprudence and betaken myself to the larger sphere of mind and morals. Men are cast iron, but children are wax . . . I devote myself to the supremest welfare of mankind upon earth. I have faith in the improvability of the race—in their accelerating improvability."

He covered the state from end to end, holding what he called "revival meetings" to discuss the public schools, their problems and their hopes. He firmly believed that each state must take responsibility for the education of children, must set standards for community action, and must see to it that equal opportunities were available to all children, regardless of their station in life. "In a government like ours," he said, "each individual must think of the welfare of all as well as the welfare of his own family, and therefore of the children of others as well as his own."

Horace Mann's annual reports were, in effect, battles in the endless war for better schools and better teaching. He traveled throughout Europe, comparing teaching methods and equipment, and brought back many new theories in education.

Not all of his ideas were popular. He was attacked on all sides—by politicians, by schoolteachers, by clergymen, by editors. Such attacks had little effect on his labors, and certainly they kept education in the public eye. During his dozen years of educational leadership in Massachusetts the financial support of public schools doubled, teachers' salaries were greatly increased, the school year lengthened, three state normal schools were established, dozens of grade schools and high schools were built, and school libraries were popularized. He was tireless in his travels and speaking engagements, and his influence extended far beyond the limits of his statutory authority.

Walter Hines Page was a direct spiritual heir to Holbrook and Mann, with the South as his special vineyard. His crusade for public education there was ably carried forward by two educational statesmen, Dr. Charles D. McIver of Greensboro, North Carolina, and Edwin A. Alderman, later president of the University of Virginia. These two men literally stumped the countryside "in an attempt to arouse their lethargic countrymen to the duty of laying a small tax to save their children from illiteracy." McIver founded the State Normal College for Women to train teachers of a new generation of Southerners. Page's address there in 1897, with its provocative title, "The Forgotten Man," gave the cause of Southern education a phrase which summed up the crusade for which Page, McIver and Alderman were working.

That crusade has borne wonderful fruit in fifty years.

Today the nation may look to the South for inspiration in solving school problems. The truth is that, of all the country, the South has made the most progress in public education since 1900, and is still pushing ahead with special attention to equalizing facilities for Negroes.

The figures detailing the advances in public education in Mr. Page's native state of North Carolina since the turn of the century are literally fantastic. In 1900 there were only some thirty public high schools in the state, with about 2,000 students. Now there are nearly a thousand, with an enrollment of 188,000 students. The value of school property has increased from some $1,100,000 fifty years ago to a current figure of $231,000,000. Annual school expenditures have grown from just over $1,000,000 to more than $140,000,000. The average teacher's salary was $83.05 in 1900. Now it is $2,832. The average school term in 1900 was 71 days; now each child attends school for 180 days per year.

Page was one of the first to realize that universal education circumscribed by the Three R's would not suffice to produce a useful population. Said Mr. Page: "The schools must do something more than teach the Three R's, for a people without diversified occupations and without training do not care for the Three R's, nor do the Three R's profit them greatly. An idle and unproductive man is no less useless because he can read and write." Today this thesis is generally accepted throughout the country, and now we expect our public schools to train our young people with increasing skills and greater understanding of the responsibilities they face.

Today the demands made upon our schools far outrun their capacity to meet them. The cost of public education has grown geometrically in recent years: the fantastic increase in the number of pupils, the expansion of the fields of study in all directions, the higher standards for teachers, the greatly increased costs of construction, the effect of inflation generally—all these have combined to push the costs of education higher and higher. And it has been estimated that in the next seven years the country will need six hundred thousand new classrooms, at a cost of twenty billion dollars.

How can we afford to provide all of this money, needed so urgently by our schools?

How can we afford *not* to provide all that is required?

Holbrook and Mann and Page, together with hundreds and thousands of unsung heroes in the fight for good education, saw clearly that our survival as a nation depended in great degree upon the creation of an intelligent, educated populace. That was never more true than it is today.

Every argument that Walter Page advanced in the

three speeches in this little book applies as pertinently to the total American educational scene today as it did to the South fifty years ago. Here is stated the fundamental case for universal education, dramatized against a pioneer backdrop.

Today the backdrop has changed. But the problems are still with us. And the same actors read essentially the same lines. We find today the same autocratic traditionalists, the same lethargic men of good will.

It is the good fortune of our schools and our nation that we find also men cast in the mold of Mr. Page, men of the same practical wisdom and crusading spirit, willing and eager to give of their time and their energies on behalf of the public schools. There are men like John Lapp of Chicago, who led his fellow citizens in their successful fight to exile politics from that city's school system. There is Henry Toy of Wilmington, Delaware, who organized the citizens of his state to get better schools and who left a promising career with the du Pont Company to accept a position as executive director of the National Citizens Commission for the Public Schools. There is Edward Tuttle, the executive secretary of the National School Boards Association, who serves education by awakening members of school boards to a fuller sense of their opportunities and responsibilities. There is James McClure of Asheville, North Carolina, whose work on behalf of the schools of Walter

Page's native state has recently received nationwide acclaim.

In addition to such men whose work has attracted public attention, there are hundreds and thousands of individual citizens now actively working for the schools of their own communities. During the last three years the National Citizens Commission for the Public Schools has seen the organization of more than 1,700 special local committees organized for the purpose of ensuring the best possible education for the children of their communities. The number increases daily.

More and more responsible citizens, men and women from every walk of life, every political persuasion, every profession or occupation, every religious faith and every social group, are joining with their neighbors to work for the good of their schools. This spirit of community cooperation and participation is an exciting thing to see and it is producing exciting results for the community as a whole as well as for the schools.

Mr. Page wrote more than fifty years ago of "The School That Built a Town," and his thesis of the beneficial effect on the community exerted by a good school has equal validity today in many towns and cities. We have seen again and again the pride and self-respect of a community regenerated through responsible citizen activity on behalf of the schools.

An awakened community is one in which individuals have begun to realize their responsibility and their strength. When such action develops, something exciting, new and good is already working to strengthen the life of that community. Its spirit has already been lifted —something has happened to it—there is a new sense of pride, of heightened community self-respect. Its citizens have seen a vision of the better life that is within their reach.

If we now envision a world of peace and understanding, a world in which all men may live in freedom and dignity, we must first make that vision a reality in our own nation, our own state, our own community.

If we believe in freedom, freedom with responsibility, then we must believe in equality of opportunity as a basic axiom of that freedom.

If we believe in equality of opportunity, then we must ask that our tax-supported system of public schools provide equal educational advantages for all of our youngsters. For here in our system of public education is one way we can give practical and concrete expression to our faith in equality of opportunity. Here is one practical way to perpetuate for future generations of Americans the good fortune we have enjoyed as the heritage of our wise Founding Fathers who, as of their day, saw all this so clearly.

this awakened community is one in which individuals have learned to make their responsibilities seem less through. When such acting is done, something extra has been put back already working to strengthen the whole community. Its spirit has already been lifted—something had happened to it—there is a new sense of pride of heightened community self-respect. Its citizens have seen a vision of the better life that is within their reach.

It we can envision a world of peace and understanding, a world in which all men can live in freedom and dignity, we must first make that vision a reality in our own nation, our own state, our own community.

If we believe in freedom, teaches with responsibility then we must believe in equality of opportunity as a basic human of that freedom.

If we believe in equality of opportunity, then we must ask that our tax-supported system of public schools provide equal educational advantages for all of our youngsters. For here in our system of public education is one way we can give practical and concrete expression to our faith in equality of opportunity. Here is one practical way to make sure for future generations of Americans the good fortune we have enjoyed as the heritage of our wise, foresighted Forefathers who at that day saw all this so clearly.

The Forgotten Man

[*An address delivered at the State Normal and Industrial School for Women at Greensboro, North Carolina, June 1897*]

THE CORDIALITY OF YOUR GREETING TOUCHES ME deeply. I have not, as some old-time wanderers are said to have done, carried with me wherever I have gone a pot of my native earth; but I have carried with me always what the pot of earth would stand for. Your welcome is the more gratifying because you are kind enough to link me with the great cause for which your institution stands.

We have often reminded ourselves and informed other people that we have incalculable undeveloped resources in North Carolina, in our streams, our forests, our mines, our quarries, our soil—that Nature has been most bountiful; so that our undeveloped resources invite men under the pleasantest conditions to productive industry. And so they do. But there is one undeveloped resource more valuable than all these, and that is the people themselves. It is about the development of men that I shall speak, more particularly about the development of forgotten and neglected men.

In making an estimate of a civilization it is the neglected and forgotten man more than any other that must be taken into account. When you build a house, you make the foundation the strongest part of it, and the house, however ornate its architecture, can be no stronger than the foundation. In considering the level of the life of any community, you must not give undue value to any class of men. A community is not rich because it contains a few rich men, it is not healthful because it contains a few strong men, it is not intelligent because it contains a few men of learning, nor is it of good morals because it contains good women—if the rest of the population also be not well-to-do, or healthful, or intelligent, or of good morals. The common people is the class most to be considered in the structure of civilization. Moreover, in proportion as any community in the organization of its society or in the development of its institutions lays emphasis on its few rich men, or its few cultivated men, it is likely to forget and to neglect its very foundations. It is not these small classes that really make the community what it is, that determine the condition of its health, the soundness of its social structure, its economic value and its level of life. The security and the soundness of the whole body are measured at last by the condition of its weakest part.

So much, if you please, to get the proper point of view. If you have been in the habit in your social studies of dividing men into classes and of considering some more important in possibilities to the common weal than others, your studies are not in keeping with the dominant democracy of our country and of our race. In any scheme of man-culture one man must be regarded of as great importance as another. The doctrine of equality of opportunity is at the bottom of social progress, for you can never judge a man's capacity except as he has opportunity to develop it. When we make a social study, we must come face to face with all the men who make up the social body, seeing them as they are, and not through the medium of our traditions nor by their estimates of themselves.

From this point of view let me make a very rapid and general survey of the culture of men in North Carolina—of the social structure and the social forces that have shaped our civilization.

In the days of our fathers the social structure was to a slight extent aristocratic, but it was much less aristocratic than the social structure was, for example, in Virginia or in South Carolina. The mass of the people were common people; they lived directly out of the soil and they had the manners and the virtues and the limitations of a simple agricultural population, which was much the same in the early part of the century in all countries where a livelihood was easily obtained. They were nearly all of English and Scotch, and Scotch-Irish stock. Most of them were sprung from peasants of sturdy qualities; a very few from gentlemen; and some were descended from forced and hired immigrants. Taken all together they were a common people, capable of as sound development as the population of any other State. But they were ignorant, as the common people in all lands were a hundred years ago.

The dominant idea of education was that it was a luxury for the rich, or a privilege of the well-born—if a necessity at all, a necessity only for the ruling class. This class-feeling in education was perceptible even within my recollection. When I was a pupil at the most famous school for boys in the State, a lad whose father had not had a military or political career was at a certain disadvantage. I recall a scene more ludicrous than any in Dickens when a thirteen-year-old companion of mine came to my room one day, shut the door and fell on the bed and wept—because his father was not a Colonel. I tried to comfort him by telling him that my father was not a Colonel either. So far from consoling him this information only gave him the less respect for me. I had not seen this weeping lad for more than twenty-five years, till I recently met him on the train. He was telling me of his children and I asked if he had ever reflected that his own children's father was not a Colonel. He recalled the incident as clearly as I recalled it. Learning might be acquired but there could be no true education in an atmosphere where such an incident could happen.

These things I mention not in blame of our ancestors. It is out of just such stock that the men came who to-day rule the world. But I mention these things because we ourselves have written and spoken such nonsense about ourselves and about our ancestors and have made ourselves believe we were in some way different from other sturdy folk and that we were in some way better than other common people. Thus we have come to put a false value on our social structure, and we have never looked ourselves in the face and seen ourselves as others see us. This false view has done incalculable hurt. All social progress must begin with a clear understanding of men as they are. We are all common folk, then, who were once dominated by a little aristocracy, which, in its social and economic character, made a failure and left a stubborn crop of wrong social notions behind it—especially about education.

There lingers one very striking relic of the aristocratic structure of opinion in North Carolina—a certain timidity on the part of our leaders in dealing with the public, a timidity on the part of the leaders, which we have falsely called conservatism on the part of the people, a hesitation to trust the people's judgment. It cropped out humorously on this platform yesterday.

Mr. Scarborough declared that our people were conservative—very conservative! You must consider what they are ready for and what they are not ready for, for they are very conservative. A half hour later, while narrating the career of Dorothea Dix, Mr. Carr showed how one woman of enthusiasm came here from Massachusetts and induced the State to spend for a single institution at one time (and that an asylum for the insane) a larger sum than the whole annual resources of the State government; and on man has from that day to this made objection to the expenditure. Our whole history is full of such incidents. Almost every noteworthy thing that we have done has been done in obedience to an impulse. Conservative? We are the most impulsive people imaginable. But if "conservatism" so overcome anyone who hears me in the very conservative things that I have to say, it must be understood that I speak only for myself. I speak out of my own ignorance only, and I speak, I regret to say, only as a spectator of your noble work.

In the old days when education was dominated by the aristocratic idea, the chief influences that shaped opinion were the stump and pulpit. From the stump two cardinal articles of faith were proclaimed. One was that a man must have liberty. Much was made of what was called personal liberty, and I think rightly. If any man sought an unfair advantage of another, the injured man was quick to assert his rights before the law, if, indeed, he did not assert it with his fists. This sturdy notion of liberty has been a great quality from the time of the Mecklenburg Declaration till to-day. If our fathers emphasized it too much let us forgive them, for we shall see presently that we also have need of some fighting qualities. Another article of faith proclaimed from the stump was that taxes were too high. From the days of King George to this day, the politicians of North Carolina have declaimed against taxes, thus laying the foundation of our poverty. It was a misfortune for us that the quarrel with King George happened to turn on a question of taxation—so great was the dread of taxation that was instilled into us.

The other great educational force was the pulpit. Parts of the people were strongly inclined to an emotional kind of religion, and our historians tell us of great camp meetings and "revivals" that swept over whole counties, continued for weeks, and threw many persons into trances. More men lost their reason from religious troubles than from any other cause, except the lonely overwork of women. The latest book written and published in the State that I have happened to see is the autobiography of a notable religious maniac whom I knew in my boyhood. The more primitive and violent forms of religion took a deep hold on the people and (as is usually the case) without affecting their conduct at all.

Not only was the preacher a mighty man in our life, but there was in the old days a type of preacher who was an heroic man, a man who had all the qualities of the pioneer. He was ready any day to face the hardships of the wilderness or to stand in the presence of the Almighty. I doubt if we have ever produced other men as great as our pioneer preachers. They were cast in so large a mould, they dealt so directly with the fundamental emotions of men and with some of the great facts of the spiritual life, that they almost ranged themselves with the giants. I had rather have known one of these men than all the political and military heroes that we have since bred. The politician has been the greater popular hero, but the preacher has had much the greater influence. For a century he was by far our greatest man —the man of the largest original power and of the strongest character. He inherited the heroic qualities of the pioneers, and he led a life at once serene and active. He was a primitive sort of character, genuine and fearless. If our traditions overrate the political leaders that we have produced, they as greatly underrate the early preachers.

Now let us see what these two powers that ruled our fathers did for the education of the masses. The first conception of education was the aristocratic conception, and the first system of teaching was controlled by those who held political power; it was the old system of class education. It did not touch the masses. They had no part in it. They grew up with the idea that education was a special privilege: they did not aspire to it, did not believe that it was attainable, and at last they came to believe that it was not desirable, certainly that it was not necessary. They remained illiterate, neglected, forgotten. There was no substantial progress in broadening educational opportunities in North Carolina from the time of the colony till the beginning of the civil war, except the noteworthy and noble work that was done just before the war to develop a public school system. This notable and noteworthy effort give us good reason to hold those who made it, chief among whom was Calvin H. Wiley, in grateful remembrance.

I commend to you most earnestly as of the first importance a thorough study of our social beginnings and development—not always as it has been described by our historians, but from original sources. You will clear your minds of the hazy exaggerations that we get from tradition. Many traditional heroes will disappear, and many whose names have been forgotten or are seldom heard will re-appear as real heroes. Among these will be the group of men who strove forty years ago or more to establish a public school system. But their scheme, like Jefferson's own great scheme, was doomed to await a later time for its development.

Later than the aristocratic system of education, and overlapping it, came the ecclesiastical system. In establishing and developing this, the preachers did valiant service. They were colporteurs and they carried religious books to the people. The churches established, besides preparatory schools for boys and girls, three schools for men which grew into colleges. At first they were established for the education of preachers, but they broadened their field of labour and became schools of general culture, and most admirable service they have done. The denominational educational movement was broader in its benefits than the old aristocratic educational movement had been, for these colleges were open to the common people and they proclaimed the desirability of general education. Still they were class institutions; each was a school of a sect. Universal education, universal free education, was not on their programme. Some men whom the State had neglected were now remembered by the churches, especially if they were of an emotional temperament and felt "called" to preach. The way towards general education was broadening, but the very conception of education was yet a class conception. It was provided less for the sake of the people than for the sake of the church.

The forgotten man remained forgotten. The aristocratic scheme of education had passed him by. To a less extent, but still to the extent of hundreds of thousands, the ecclesiastical scheme also passed him by. The general level of education was almost as low as it had ever been. Both the aristocratic and the ecclesiastical plans held undisputed sway till a time within the memory of us all. But in the meantime education had been making more rapid conquests—developing in method and extending its benefits in other States and in other lands—than in any preceding time in the history of the world.

Tried by the tests of this progress, what have the aristocratic system and the ecclesiastical system of education to show for themselves?

First, what did they do for their own favoured classes? North Carolina is one of the old thirteen States. The aristocratic system had free play here for nearly a hundred years, and the ecclesiastical system has had free play for at least half as long. They established our university and our denominational colleges. Excellent as these are, they do not rank with the best institutions of most of the other original thirteen States—or Virginia, nor of New Jersey, nor of New York, nor of Connecti-

cut, nor of Massachusetts. Nor have they trained even a
select body of scholars that have been or are in any way
famous. Make another test: there are no great libraries
in the State, nor do the people yet read, nor have the
publishing hounses yet reckoned them as their patrons,
except the publishers of school books. By any test that may
be made, both these systems of education failed even
with the classes that they appealed to. One such test
is the test of emigration from the State. In 1890 there
were living in other States 293,000 persons who were
born in North Carolina. One in eight of every native of
the State then living had gone away. When we remember that almost every one of those emigrants went to
States where taxes are higher and schools are more
numerous and better and where competition is more
fierce, and when we remember that they went away from
a State that is yet sparsely settled and richer in natural
opportunities than most of the States to which they
went, the failure of these systems becomes painfully
obvious.

If a slave brought $1,000 in old times, it ought to be
safe to assume that every emigrant from the State has an
economic value of $1,000. This emigration therefore
had up to 1890 cost us $293,000,000—a fact that goes
far to explain why we are poor. To take the places of
these 293,000 emigrants, after twenty years of organized

effort to induce immigration 52,000 immigrants born in other States had come here, a large proportion of whom had come for their health. By counting the sick and the dying at $1,000 each, we had still lost $241,000,000 by the transaction. This calculation gives a slight hint of the cost of ignorance and of the extravagance of keeping taxes too low.

Next, what did these systems of education do for the masses? In 1890, twenty-six per cent. of the white persons of the State were unable even to read and write. One in every four was wholly forgotten. But illiteracy was not the worst of it; the worst of it was that the stationary social condition indicated by generations of illiteracy had long been the general condition. The forgotten man was content to be forgotten. He became not only a dead weight, but a definite opponent of social progress. He faithfully heard the politicians on the stump praise him for virtues that he did not have. The politicians told him that he lived in the best State in the Union, told him that the other politician had some harebrained plan to increase his taxes, told him as a consolation for his ignorance how many of his kinsmen had been killed in the war, told him to distrust anybody who wished to change anything. What was good enough for his fathers was good enough for him. Thus the forgotten man became a dupe, became thankful for being neglected. And the preacher told him that the ills and misfortunes of this life were blessings in disguise, that God meant his poverty as a means of grace, and that if he accepted the right creed all would be well with him. These influences encouraged inertia. There could not have been a better means to prevent the development of the people.

I have thus far spoken only of the forgotten man. I have done so to show the social and educational structure in proper perspective. But what I have come to speak about is the forgotten woman. Both the aristocratic and the ecclesiastical systems made provision for the women of special classes—the fortunately born and the religious well-to-do. But all the other women were forgotten. Let any man whose mind is not hardened by some worn-out theory of politics or of ecclesiasticism go to the country in almost any part of the State and make a study of life there, especially of the life of the women. He will see them thin and wrinkled in youth from ill prepared food, clad without warmth or grace, living in untidy houses, working from daylight till bed-time at the dull round of weary duties, the slaves of men of equal slovenliness, the mothers of joyless children—all uneducated if not illiterate. Yet even their condition were endurable if there were any hope, but this type of woman is encrusted in a shell of dull content with her lot; she knows no better and can never learn better, nor point her children to a higher life. If she be intensely religious, her religion is only an additional misfortune, for it teaches her, as she understands it, to be content with her lot and all its burdens, since they prepare her for the life to come. Some *men* who are born under these conditions escape from them; a *man* may go away, go where life offers opportunities, but the women are forever helpless.

And this sight every one of you has seen, not in the countries whither we send missionaries, but in the borders of the State of North Carolina, in this year of grace. Nor is it an infrequent sight. There are thousands and thousands of such women in our population.

Now one of the two things is true—either these forgotten men and women are incapable of development, and belong to a lower order of intelligence than any other people of Anglo-Saxon stock; or our civilization, so far as they are concerned, has been a failure. Of course there is no doubt which of these suppositions is true; for these people are capable of development, capable of unlimited growth and elevation. But, if they be capable of development, then both the aristocratic and the ecclesiastical systems of society have failed to develop them.

Since both the politician and the preacher have failed

to lift this life after a century of unobstructed opportunities, it is time for a wiser statesmanship and a more certain means of grace. And surely of all people the preacher and the politician ought, in common modesty, to be the last to oppose a new system of education for the development of the undeveloped masses.

But now the story brightens. These old educational systems having failed here, as they have failed in other States, the public-spirited, far-sighted and energetic young men, chief among them your own President and the President of the University, who came into activity ten years or more ago, began seriously to develop a public school system, first of course in the towns. They developed by their own earnestness the work that had been in part planned by men like Major Finger. One town followed another, levying a local tax to supplement the State tax. I doubt if such an educational revival was ever known in any other State, certainly nothing like it was ever known before in North Carolina. I am sure that you who have lived here continuously for the last ten years do not know how great the quickening of civilization has been. The level of life has been moved further upward in these ten years than it was moved in any preceding fifty years. I never come here but I am astonished at the changes I hear of. The civilization that you have to-day is different from the civilization of my own boyhood by a greater remove than that civilization was different from the civilization of fifty years before.

In my judgment there has been no other event in North Carolina since the formation of the American Union that is comparable in importance to this new educational progress. The movement now has such momentum that nothing can hinder the complete development of the public school system till every child is reached. When every inhabited township votes a local tax to supplement the State tax, the taxes you now levy will seem small and will be increased. According to the last published reports of the Commissioner of Education, the total sum spent per year per pupil in the public schools was still lower in North Carolina than in any States except South Carolina. It was only $3.40. In Georgia it was nearly $6.50, in Virginia it was nearly $9, in Indiana it was $20, in Michigan nearly $20, in Wisconsin $21, in Minnesota nearly $30, in the new State of North Dakota it was nearly $33.50—nearly ten times the expenditure per pupil that was made in North Carolina. None of these States is richer than your own in possibilities. The ability to maintain schools is in proportion rather to the appreciation of education than to the amount of wealth. We pay for schools not so much out of our purses as out of our state of mind. For example, there is a man in Moore County who had two children at school at the expense of somebody else. Although he did not pay their bills, he took them from school the other day because, he said, the charge for tuition was too high. He is the frankest and most faithful believer of our old-time economic creed that I have ever known.

As the movement to establish public schools everywhere gathers force, men of wealth will find that they can do no public service with their money so sure to bring lasting results as to build schoolhouses. The history of philanthropy shows that no public benefaction brings the same sure and permanent results as provision for the free education of the masses. The battle will be practically won when the whole States shall stand on this platform:

A public school system generously supported by public sentiment, and generously maintained by both State and local taxation, is the only effective means to develop the forgotten man, and even more surely the only means to develop the forgotten woman.

Even ten years ago, many men in North Carolina did not stand on this platform. Now I hear that few oppose such a programme, and those few you will soon educate for sheer pity.

Standing in this institution to-day, it seems incredible that I myself can recall the opposition both of political

leaders and of ecclesiastical leaders to free public schools.
Nothing else ever made me so nearly hopeless. Thank
Heaven, that opposition is passed. Or, if it be not wholly
passed, and if any dupe of an old political fallacy say that
we are too poor to increase our taxes for education, remember that the average amount paid now by every taxpayer is only $2.13; the average amount paid by each
taxpayer in the poor State of Maine is $9.23; in Vir-
ginia $4.72, in Florida $5.93; in Iowa it is $15. Too poor
to maintain schools? The man who says it is the per-
petuator of poverty. It is the doctrine that has kept us
poor. It smells of the alms-house and the hovel. It has
driven more men and more wealth from the State and
kept more away than any other political doctrine ever
cost us—more even than the doctrine of Secession. Such
a man is the victim of an ancient and harmful false-
hood.

If any beggar for a church school oppose a local tax
for schools or a higher school tax, take him to the huts
of the forgotten women and children, and in their hopeless presence remind him that the church system of
education has not touched tens of thousands of these
lives, and ask him whether he think it wrong that the
Commonwealth should educate them. If he think it
wrong, ask him and ask the people plainly, whether he
be a worthy preacher of the gospel that declares one man

equal to another in the sight of God? Is not one man equal to another also in the sight of the Commonwealth? In all reasonableness, it is impossible to understand how any man can regard it as a Christian act to stand in the way of the State's elevating the neglected masses. Can any church afford to put itself in such a position? or, if it do, has it any right to complain if good men declare it an unchristian attitude? Even if you could respect the religion of the man who objects to the elevation of the forgotten masses by public education, it is hard to respect his common sense; for does his church not profit by the greater enlightenment and prosperity that every educated community enjoys? This doctrine smells of poverty —poverty in living, poverty in thinking, poverty in the spiritual life.

The most sacred thing in the Commonwealth and to the Commonwealth is the child, whether it be your child or the child of the dull-faced mother of the hovel. The child of the dull-faced mother may, for all you know, be the most capable child in the State. At its worst, it is capable of good citizenship and a useful life, if its intelligence be quickened and trained. Several of the strongest personalities that were ever born in North Carolina were men whose very fathers were unknown. We have all known two such, who held high places in church and state. President Eliot said a little while ago that the ablest man that he had known in his many years' connection with Harvard University was the son of a brick mason. The child, whether it have poor parents or rich parents, is the most valuable undeveloped resource of the State.

But the day is past when worn-out theories hold us in captivity, and we owe its passing chiefly to the idea that this institution stands for. Our whole life will soon be delivered from the bondage of ignorance by our hitherto forgotten women. I am reminded of the story of the saving of a captured city by its gentlewomen. In an old translation of Montaigne it runs thus:

> The Emperor, Conradus, third of that name, having besieged Guelphe, Duke of Bavaria, what vile or base satisfaction soever was offered him, would yield to no other milder conditions, but only to suffer such gentle women as were with the Duke in the city (their honours safe) to issue out the town afoote, with such things as they could carry about them. They, with unrelenting courage, advised and resolved themselves (neglecting all their riches or jewels to carry their husbands, their children and the Duke himselfe, on their backs. The Emperor, perceiving the quaintnesse of their device, tooke so great pleasure in it that he wept for joy, and forthwith converted the former inexorable rage and mortall hatred he bare the Duke into so milde a relenting and gentle kindnesse, that thence he entreated both him and his, with all favour and courtesy.

You that know me will bear witness that I have not spoken of our fathers, nor of our political leaders, least of all of our religious leaders, in a spirit of ungrateful criticism. I have meant with all proper respect for them and for their good qualities and good works only to show that their systems have proved failures for our needs. Doubtless under the conditions of their lives they did the best they could do. But the conditions of our lives are different; and our duty is to accept our own conditions without illusions, to face our own problems like men, and when necessary with all respect for the past to lift dead men's hands from our life.

May I go forward a step further in the development of public education that must in due time follow this delivery from the bondage of the old systems? The extension of free preparatory schools in every part of the State is leading to the establishment of free high schools, such as already exist in some towns, as in Greensboro and in Durham, and in other larger towns. These will draw to themselves the intellectual interests of the whole community and make the public school system the pride of our people. I know towns where every enlightening interest centres in the high school. Lectures are given there in literature and on music and on practical subjects as well, by the most learned men and women. Parents pursue courses of study with their children. The whole life of such towns is lifted to a high intellectual level. In some such towns private schools exist only to train those boys and girls who are too dull or backward to keep pace with the rest—a sort of asylums for the stupid. My own sons are to-day preparing to enter Harvard University at the Cambridge Latin school, where the sons and daughters of the professors at Harvard are in the same classes, or may be, with the sons and daughters of draymen and hack-drivers. All have the same privileges and the same opportunities; and no pupil can buy even a book or a pencil; the city supplies them all. Every man pays for it in his taxes; and every man profits by it in the increased value of his property, in the higher wages he receives, as a higher and higher degree of skill in all work is developed, and a higher and higher level of trained life is reached. On their way home from school these pupils may stop at a magnificent public library and take from it any book they please free of charge, or spend the day in the large reading rooms, investigating any subject they may be interested in. So may any man or woman or child in the whole city, free of charge. The library building was the gift of a wealthy citizen. The books are paid for by my taxes and the taxes of other men there. Every town in Massachusetts, but about a dozen small and remote towns, has such a free library—the direct growth of a public school system. The States of New York and Michigan send travelling libraries of new books—collections of good literature—to any town that asks for them and has a public library of its own. After these hundred or two volumes have remained in one town the allotted time, they are sent on to another, and so on indefinitely—all at the State's expense.

When I have seen these things and profited by them, and when I know that men are every day going away from this old land that they love to get such advantages for themselves and for their children, can I listen to the mendicant whine of any ignorant political or ecclesiastical leader who says that my children had better not be educated at all if they cannot be bred with his narrow outlook on life?

Now look a little further yet along the line of development of the public school system. Following the high school may come (and I think ought to come), a still higher extension of State education—the wholly free University and Industrial Schools. When your University was established, the old political idea of education prevailed, and a restricted number of boys from each country was admitted free—and these only. This system discriminates in favour of a restricted number of youths and against all the rest. It is still only a partially free system. There is always a danger that the boys who pay, if it be known who they are, will regard those who do not pay as charity students. If all alike were free—as all in my judgment ought to be—no such danger could arise.

The old aristocratic system had a leaning towards charity as the ecclesiastical system has; and the view of education as a charity has always been one of the greatest weaknesses of both systems. Education pays the State. The more persons educated the better education pays the State. But to dole it out to a restricted number is to regard it as charity and to turn the State into an alms-giver. Most of the Eastern States, where the aristocratic idea was strongest, have stopped short of free universities; but many of the Western States have been wiser.

In the State of Michigan, for instance, a child of either sex many begin its education at a public school and pursue it through the State University without charge; and this University has become one of the strongholds of learning in the Union and one of our great schools. A similar system has been adopted in Kansas, in Texas, and in other States. Any child in any one of those great Commonwealths may have free training from infancy to maturity—free training in one of the most efficient systems of education ever devised by man. And this system has been constructed and developed almost within the lifetime of the youngest of us.

The opportunity exists in North Carolina to establish

a similar system by a single effort and without any considerable increase of expenditure. We have our State University, most useful and vigorous under its recent President, and its present one, and we have our three larger and older denominational colleges—Davidson College with its solidity and old-time dignity, Wake Forest College, a striking demonstration of what people of moderate means may at any time do when they work with united purpose, and Trinity College with its new life made possible by its generous benefactors. We have all these and the other State schools and denominational schools for boys and for girls. If they could all be united into one great school, it would at once become by far the most efficient and noteworthy institution in the South. And there is no reason why it should not become one of the great seats of learning in the Union. If the doors of such an institution were thrown open free to every boy and girl in the State, and there were free schools to train them for it, we should no longer talk of forgotten men and women; and people from other States would seek homes here. These counties would be peopled at last by as useful and as cultivated a population as any in the United States.

Nor need the religious influence of any of the denominational colleges suffer by such a move when the time for it comes. Every one might have its own dormitory

and religious supervision over pupils of its own sect.
A definite movement of this sort has already been made
where the denominational schools have shown a wish
to become a part of the system of public education.

But I have wandered too far from the problems of
the immediate present. Such things as I have spoken of,
we may look for in the future. What may we not look for
in the future? Whatever I might say in prophecy would
be as inadequate as all that I might say in congratula-
tion. Great changes come as silently as the seasons. I am
no more sure of this spring time than I am of the rejuven-
ation of our society and the lifting up of our life. A
revolution is in progress, and this institution is one of the
first and best fruits of it. I declare in truth and soberness
that this is the most inspiring sight that I have ever seen
in North Carolina, for before the moral earnestness of
well-trained women social illusions vanish and worn-out
traditions fall away.

O earnest young Womanhood of the Commonwealth,
we that had forgotten you now thankfully do you honour.
Many a man with the patriotic spirit that is our inherit-
ance has striven to lift dead men's hands from our stag-
nant life and has been baffled by a century's inertia.
I speak the gladdest speech of my life when I say that
you have lifted them. This institution and your presence
is proof that the State has remembered the forgotten

woman. You in turn will remember the forgotten child; and in this remembrance is laid the foundation of a new social order. The neglected people will rise and with them will rise all the people.

The School That Built a Town

[An address delivered at the Commencement of the State Normal School at Athens, Ga., December 11, 1901]

I HEARTILY THANK YOU FOR YOUR INVITATION TO COME here; for I think that your school stands for as useful work as any work done in the world.

The training of children in the public schools gives exercise to the highest qualities—sympathy, self-sacrifice, the love of every human creature and the love of our country. These are the virtues that make men and women strong and lovely.

Your work also brings results of the highest value. The American people of this generation are a people of great practical skill; but the American people of the next generation, the Georgians among them if you do your task well, will be the most efficient people on the earth.

Your work, too, is free from doubt. There is work that men must do without enthusiasm. There is work that brings only the unrelieved weariness of toil and a plodding gait. But the direct value of what you do is free from doubt in all sound minds; for you are building the noblest fabric of society, which is a world-conquering trained democracy. Whatever others may be doing, then, you are working with the central secret of human progress; and it is an inspiration to see you.

And now, if I can repay you at all, it must be by telling you the story of the school that built a town.

It is the town of Northwood. Its early history is like the early history of hundreds of other American towns. The people who lived there were merchants, lawyers, preachers, doctors; a rich man or two; a few men that had worshops and those that worked for them: carpenters, clerks, labourers, a few loafers, a few rum sellers—the same kind of population that you could find almost anywhere in the Union. They were people of sturdy stock and good qualities. Most of them were of American parentage; but there were Germans, Irish, Jews and two Frenchmen—one a dancing master, who taught fencing also, and the other a teacher of his language. And life went on there as life goes on in all such communities. The people were pretty well-off. When court was in session many countrymen came to town, and all the loafers gathered about the court-house, and the lawyers gave the hotel an air of importance as if it were a big hotel in a big town. The farmers filled the market place on Saturday and the stores and the grog-shops drove a thriving trade. But the savings bank had many depositors, the churches were well filled on Sunday, and the Sunday-schools swarmed with pretty children; for it was a town of large families.

And there were schools of course. One was kept by a good lady who had studied French and music in her youth and who held on in her widowhood to the memories of her triumphs which still threw a gentle halo over her. She taught at her home a group of the best-bred children of the town. She taught them to speak with a certain prim correctness, and at the end of every term she coached them to stand in their pretty frocks and clean breeches in a pretty row and to recite pretty verses and to make a pretty bow to their mothers. They took home good reports and their parents said that they were very fortunate to have so cultivated a lady to teach their children.

There was another school kept by another lady. She was young and energetic and she put emphasis on modern methods of education. She had the real Frenchman to teach French. She laid great stress on calisthenics and she put on gymnasium clothes herself and led the children in their exercises. She was a young woman of great physical vigour, and naturally the children of strenuous parents came to her school and they boasted that she made it her business to teach, not to confer a social distinction on her pupils.

Then there was a school for boys at which they were

prepared for business or for college, and it was a good academy of the old sort. Two men owned and conducted it. One was an old-fashioned scholar who made the boys learn the Latin grammar by heart, and who flogged them when they failed; and he was looked upon as men afar off look upon stern Learning. If you could have taken the popular conception of the Higher Education, clothed it in flesh and put a plug hat on it, you would have had that man. If you had met him in the street for the first time, you would have known his calling and could have guessed his history; for he had won prizes at the university in his classical studies. It was sometimes said that he recited Horace to himself with his eyes shut while he pretended to look at the boys play baseball. His partner was a bookkeeper and a business man who taught the boys that were taking the commercial course to keep accounts and to write a plain hand; and he taught the English branches also. The boys who attended this school were the sons of the best-to-do families of the town, and there were boarding pupils too.

Then still another school was established in Northwood when the town had grown a little bigger. This was a seminary for young ladies, and it was a church-school. A preacher and his wife were the principals; and, besides the girls that lived in the town, a good many came from

that it had been ten years before. Yet important changes had been going on, and the most important was the change in the public school. It became so crowded with the children of the poorer class that it was necessary to build a second school-house. This was built in the end of the town where well-to-do people lived, and more and more of them took to sending their children to it.

About that time a greater interest was taken in public school education throughout the State. The university had been made free to every pupil in the Commonwealth who was prepared to enter it, and the public school system was much talked about and developed.

It so happened that the principal of one of the public schools in Northwood at that time was an uncommonly energetic man—a man who knew how to manage men. He made a very careful study of the population, and this is what he found—that, in spite of all the schools in the town, there were a great many children that were not at school at all. There were many more of them than anybody would have believed. He found also that even those that got a smattering of book-learning got nothing else, and that few received further instruction than the schools in the town gave. He made a list of all the families in Northwood, and it filled a book almost as big as a banker's ledger. He put down in it the boys and the girls whose education was prematurely arrested. One night he sat down with the summary of this book before him, and he said to himself, "These people are not in earnest about education; they are simply playing with it and are fooling themselves."

He showed this summary first to one man, then to another. In this way first one man and then another was led to think about the subject in a new way. I need not tire you with the details of the agitation that followed; for it extended over many years. But the result was that a third public school was built. Then sometime later a high-school was built. In a few years it was found inadequate, and the building was used as still another primary public school and a larger house was put up for the high-school. By this time the public schools had ceased to be regarded as schools for the poor. They were the best schools in the town, and almost all the people in the town sent their children to them. Long ago, the old scramble about teachers had ceased. Influential citizens had stopped trying to get places for their widowed daughters-in-law and their wives' nieces in the schools because they needed work. Only well-trained teachers, as a rule, were engaged. The best men in the town served on the school-board, and they had got so tired of the scramble for places that they had a law passed by the legislature which permitted them to appoint a school director, who in turn could himself appoint teachers, and nobody else could. They held him responsible; and, since he was not elected, he had no temptation to appoint incompetent ones.

With the feeling of security, every school principal and teacher became courageous. Especially courageous was the principal of the high-school. He put a carpenter-shop in the basement which developed into a wood-working department, and he graded the pupils on their course in wood-work just as he graded them in any book-study. This pleased the people. They said that he was "practical." But he took the trouble to explain that he was not training carpenters, and he insisted that they must not misunderstand him.

But the plan was so popular that a well-to-do builder, whose son had taken a great interest in the wood-working course, gave the school a very much better shop. Then by some other stroke of good luck (I've forgotten the details of the story) a shop was added for work in iron —a little shop, almost a toy-shop; but the children were taught there. Then came a garden, for a quarter of an acre was set aside and the children learned to plant and to work things that grow. In the meantime a small chemical laboratory had been fitted up, and a physical laboratory as well. Then a separate building was given for use as a gymnasium. Somebody gave a small library. At a public meeting a year or two later it was decided to build a public library next the school-house.

Workshops, a garden, laboratories, a library, a gym-

nasium—there were other things as well. A kitchen was
built and the girls were taught to cook. Then a dozen
other things came along, such as basket-making; singing
was taught uncommonly well, and nearly all the young
people learned to sing. And the school had an orchestra.
Every boy and girl took a course of work with the hands
as well as with the head; and it was discovered that the
head-work was the better done for the hand-work.

At last a generation had grown up that had been
educated in the public schools of Northwood. Nearly
every useful man in the town and most of the useful
women were high-school graduates. They made the
social life of the town. The doctor, the dentist, the
preacher, the mayor, even the Governor, most of the
merchants, the owner of a knitting mill, the owner of
a furniture factory, the owner of a great tin-shop, the
owner of a wagon factory—all sorts of successful men
had been graduated at this school and most of them had
got the impulse there that shaped their careers.

And the high-school was both the intellectual and
the industrial centre of the town and of the region. The
scholars went there to the library; the farmers went there
to consult the chemist or the entomologist; men of almost
all crafts and callings found an authority there. For this
high-school had now become what we should call a
college and a very well organized one too.

In the first period of Northwood's history, you will observe, the town carried the schools—carried them as a burden. The schools of the cultivated widow, the strenuous young lady and the old fashioned scholar and the young ladies' seminary, much as the several sets and sects each boasted of its own institution, were really tolerated rather than generously supported. The principals had to beg for them in one form or other. The public school was regarded as a sort of orphan asylum for the poor. The whole educational work of the town was on a semi-mendicant basis; or it was half a sort of social function, half a sort of charity. It really did not touch the intellectual life of the people. *They* supported *it*. *It* did not lift *them*. The town carried the schools as social and charitable burdens.

Now this is all changed. The school has made the town. It has given nearly every successful man in it his first impulse in his career, and it has given the community great renown. Teachers from all over the country go there to see it. More than that, many pupils go from a distance to enter the high-school. More than that, men have gone there to live because of the school. They go there to establish industries of various sorts, because the best expert knowledge of every craft can be found there. The town has prospered and has been rebuilt. The architects are high-school men; the engineers who graded the streets and made a model system of sewers are high-school men; the roads were laid out by high-school men. There is a whole county of model farms and dairies and good stock farms. High-school men have in this generation made the community a new community. They conduct all sorts of factories—they make furniture, they make things of leather, they make things of wrought iron; they have hundreds of small industries. It is said that a third of the houses in the town contain home-made furniture after beautiful old patterns that the owners themselves have made. And there is one man who does inlaid work in wood. And all this activity clusters about the public schools. The high-school now not only affects but it may be said to dominate the life of the town; and this is the school that has built the town, for it has given everybody an impetus and has started nearly everybody towards an occupation. It has enabled them to find their own aptitudes.

Now there is all the difference in the world between the Northwood of this generation, and the Northwood of the generation before. It is a difference so great that it cannot be told in one morning. But the change is simply the result of a changed view of education.

Education, Ladies and Gentlemen, when it is dallied with, played with, tolerated, and imperfectly done, is a costly and troublesome thing. In the first place it is talked to death. It causes more discussion than politics or than bad crops. There are many persons who do not believe in it and many more who wish they did not and could get rid of the bother of it.

But when education becomes not only part and parcel of the life of the people, but a thing that they have all profited by—a thing that underlies life as the soil underlies the growth in the garden—then education becomes cheap and easy. Nobody asks what it costs, nobody questions its benefits, nobody harbours a doubt about it.

In one case the community grudgingly supports its schools as a burden. In the other case, the schools build the community. And this is the lesson of Northwood.

The difference between one conception of education and the other, when it dawns on a man, changes his whole attitude towards teaching and towards social problems and towards the State. He becomes another man. For one view is selfish and the other is patriotic. One undertakes to develop a few men and women and it fails because no man can be really well developed in a community of undeveloped men. This is one reason why isolated scholars are so often impracticable, and this is the reason why many business men tell you that they do not believe in college education. The other conception of education is that it trains all the members of a community and thus enables every one to find his natural aptitudes.

To carry on education as a privilege is to mistrain some

and to leave the others untrained. To carry it on as a universal duty is to open to every one his natural opportunity, to enable every one to find himself and to find his usefulness to his fellows. It is to give balance and flexibility and symmetry to the whole community.

Has any man here doubt about this? Does any man think that I am spinning a pretty theory? Does any man still hold to the notion that, if the children of the rich are sent off to college, and the children of the poor have a little "schooling" so that they can read a newspaper and calculate the cost of a bale of cotton, we shall continue to get along tolerably well? Is any man here opposed to building a good school-house in every school-district of Georgia, and to employing the best teachers in the world and to making the school a training-place for every child in the district—one for whites and one for blacks? If you hold these notions, you are a dead weight on Georgia. You are one of the reasons why its property is not now worth five times what it is. You are one of the reasons why the products of its soil are not five times as great as they are, for such schools as I mean would make most farmers highly successful farmers. You are one reason why the population of the State is not twice or thrice what it is; for such schools as I mean would attract good people from every part of the world, and cause more children to grow to healthful maturity. You are one of the reasons why Georgia is not one of the greatest manufacturing States in the Union, for such schools as I mean would turn thousands of the best-trained hands and minds to the making of beautiful and useful things. You are one of the reasons why the Georgians have not more scholars, more orators, more organizers of industry, more owners of beautiful homes, more horses and cattle and grass and fruit and more good roads and more strong men and more lovely women and more beautiful children than any other State in the Union. Last of all, you are not a democrat. You have never thoroughly read Thomas Jefferson. You do not know that his ideal State was a State in which every man was trained at the public expense. You are a frayed-out "knight" of feudal times with a faded plume and you think in terms of the Middle Ages; and the sooner you know it the better for the community, and I am glad of a chance plainly to tell you so.

Of course, Ladies and Gentlemen, there is no such man in your community. Perhaps there is no such man in all Georgia. But there are men in every community and in every State in the Union who even yet do not know the full meaning of what you are doing. For what are you doing? You are not mere teachers of children as the widow and the old scholar and the old preacher in Northwood were. You are also the builders of a new social order. The future of Georgia is in your hands. You are the high servants of the State, but for that very reason you are not the servants of any sect or party or class, and sects and parties and classes must keep their hands off you. You must be free—you of all men and women.

It falls to you to make it plain by your work and by your bearing that yours is the most patriotic and the most important service that any class gives to the State. You must stand up for what you stand for. You know what you are trying to do. Others have various vague notions of social growth. You know that there is only one true science of building a stable and broad-based democratic social structure. You know what you need for your work. Demand it as a right in the name of the children of the Commonwealth. In other words, never for a moment be afraid of that dying body of opinion which looks on the public school as a sort of educational orphan asylum. Stand to it, that it is the nursery of the leaders of the world, as by the high virtue of our invincible democracy it is!

But to return to the school at Northwood. The diploma give by the school tells something more definite than most diplomas tell, and every diploma does not tell the same thing. One recites what courses of study a boy has taken and how well he has mastered them. But it tells also that he can swim well, that he can do work in iron, that he can draw, that he has good muscles. It tells, too, that he is persistent and plucky, and that he is unselfish and thrifty. The diploma is made to fit the boy, not the boy to fit the diploma. It tells what sort of boy he is, what he has done, and what he is good for. A diploma given to a girl likewise tells frankly the character and the equipment of that particular girl; for the people of Northwood are so much in earnest about education that they have learned to be perfectly frank. The diploma will tell that the girl is of sound body, that she can sing, that she can row, and it plainly says that she has good manners; it tells her good qualities of mind and of temper, as well as the success with which she has pursued her studies. It tells that she can lay out and work a garden of roses or of potatoes. If all the diplomas given to all the graduates were the same, they would not value them.

The school, you understand, is not a mere workshop, nor is it a place to learn a trade. It does not make carpenters of boys nor cooks of girls. Nor does it make Greek scholars or poets or musicians of them. But it comes as near to making them the one thing as the other. It comes as near to making cooks and chemists and farmers as it comes to making scholars. For those high schools and colleges that teach only books and train only the mind and not the hands—*they* do not really make scholars as we used to suppose that they did. The utmost that they do it to teach the boy the rudiments of scholarship and the method of work by which, if he persist, he may some day become a scholar. This school does the same thing in scholarship, but it does also a corresponding thing in hand-work. The old kind of teachers simply fooled themselves and misled their pupils and the community when they assumed that their courses in literature and the like made scholars. And what a wasteful self-deception it was! In Northwood, one boy may, if he persist, become a scholar; another a wheelwright, another a farmer; and so on. And it is found that by doing hand-work also the pupils do better head-work as well. It simply opens to all the intellectual life and the way to useful occupations at the same time.

There are two things that they are all taught in that school. They are taught to write a plain hand-writing, and they look upon a bad hand-writing as they look upon neglect of dress—it is the mark of a sloven. And they are all taught to write the English language in short clear sentences, so that anybody can understand what they write.

Now let us see how the people of Northwood themselves look at education. The simplicity of the work of the school is what first strikes you. And you find this same simplicity in the people's conception of education. They do not call it education. They call it training. They speak of a boy as trained in Greek or in metal-work; and of a girl as trained to sing or to draw or to cook. This frank and simple way of looking at school-work has changed their whole conception of education. It has brushed away a vast amount of nonsense, and cleaned the mind of a great accumulation of cobwebs. For one thing nobody in that town makes addresses on the need of education. A man would as soon think of making an address on the necessity of the atmosphere, or of fuel, or of bread. And you never hear anything about elaborate systems of education, or the co-ordina-tion of studies, or the psychology of the unrelated.

They look at the trades and the professions in the same simple way. They say that one man has been trained as a physician, that another has been trained as a farmer, that another has been trained as a preacher, that another has been trained as a builder, another as a machinist; and they lay less stress on what a man chooses to do than upon the way in which he does it. It is respectable to have any calling you like, provided you are trained to it; but it isn't respectable to have any calling unless you are trained. The town for this reason is not divided into the same sort of sets and classes that

you find in most towns. There is not one class that puts
on airs and regards itself as the Educated Class, to
which all other classes are supposed to pay deference.
Of course some men read more books than others; some
are more cultivated than others, and there are social
divisions of the people there as there are the world over.
But when everybody knows how to do something *well*,
a man who does one thing well enjoys no particular
distinction. A jacklag lawyer can't compel any great
respect from a really scientific horseshoer. The mastery
of anything is a wonderful elevator of character and
judgment.

Next to their simple and straightforward way of looking at education what strikes you most about the people
of Northwood is their universal interest in the school.
Apparently everybody has now been trained there. But
when one man thinks of the school he thinks of the
library; another of the laboratory; another of music;
another of chemistry. Books are only one kind of tools,
and the other kinds are co-ordinate with them. And
everybody goes to the great schoolhouse more or less
often. The singers give their concerts there. I was there
once when a young man gave a performance of a musical
composition of his own, and at another time when a man
showed the first bicycle that had been made in the
town. In three months he had a bicycle factory. Every-

body is linked to the school by his work, and there is, therefore, no school party and no anti-school party in local politics. There is no social set that looks down on the school. The school built the town, and it is the town. It has grown beyond all social distinctions and religious differences and differences of personal fortune. It has united the people, and they look upon it as the training place in which everybody is interested alike, just as they look upon the court-house as the place where every man is on the same footing. The fathers of our liberties made the court-house every man's house. The equally important truth is that we must, in the same way, make the public school-house everybody's house before we can establish the right notion of education.

Now no wise man has anything to say against church schools or private schools in their right places; for both have their uses. But the history of civilization has proved over and over again that no church and no private means can ever overcome the social and financial and political and religious differences of people and build a training place for all. Nothing has ever done this and nothing ever can do it but a public institution that is maintained by taxation and that belongs to all the people alike.

And now we come to the very heart of the matter. To talk about education in a democratic country as meaning anything else than free public education for every child is a mockery. To call anything else education at all is to go back towards the Middle Ages, when it was regarded as a privilege of gentlemen or as a duty of the church and not as a necessity for the people.

If a few men only are to be educated, the accidents of fortune determine which they shall be. These will regard themselves as a special class, set off by themselves; and a false standard of education is set up both in the minds of the educated and in the minds of the uneducated. The uneducated regard themselves as neglected. You have the seeds of snobbery and of discontent sowed over all the wide wastes of social life, and the uneducated part of the State simply adds to its inertia rather than to its wealth and health.

But even this false conception of education is not the worst result of a system that benefits only a few. If only a part of any community be trained, the very part that needs training least is the part that gets it. It is the ignorant that are neglected, and the State thus goes steadily down. For those that are predisposed to ignorance and idleness and a lack of occupation are the very members of the community that ought not under any circumstances to be neglected. There is, therefore, no way under Heaven to train those who need training most but by training everybody at the public expense.

More than this (for democracy has the quality of giving constant surprises) it is always more than likely that among the neglected are those that would become the most capable if they were trained. Society forever needs reinforcements from the rear. It is a shining day in any educated man's growth when he comes to see and to know and to feel and freely to admit that it is just as important to the world that the ragamuffin child of his worthless neighbour should be trained as it is that his own child should be. Until a man sees this he cannot become a worthy democrat nor get a patriotic conception of education; for no man has known the deep meaning of democracy or felt either its obligation or its lift till he has seen this truth clearly.

There is another peculiarity about the people of Northwood that you will notice. They talk about the proper training of men, but you never hear them say much about the natural resources of their community. When I went there, I recalled that some of our Southern people used to talk much about our natural resources and to invite all the world to come and live with them, because they had good air and good water and good soil and good timber and gold and iron under the ground—in other words, because God had been generous to the land. Well, the truth is, the land was really richer when the Indians held it than it is now; the water was just as good, the air just as pure, and there were more forests and more iron and gold than there are now. For that matter there are undeveloped regions in South America that have many natural advantages even over the great and varied natural advantages of Georgia.

This programme of inviting settlers was a programme of sheer dependence on Nature. It implied the old conception of education, the old conception of wealth-creation; for it took no account or little account of the part that men play in making wealth. God might make a land as fertile as Eden and underlay it with gold and stock it with venison and quail; yet it would yield no more than men made it yield. Within reasonable limits, it matters little what Nature has done for a country. If you take any land in the temperate zone and put well-trained men there, the land will turn out to be all right. What did Nature do for Holland, which is the most densely peopled country of Europe, and one of the most thrifty and happy? Nature overflowed it with the sea, and man had to reclaim the very soil he lives on. On the other hand, the city that was the capital of the Roman Empire is now to a great degree uninhabitable for malaria and fevers, and the Grecian archipelago itself does not attract modern immigration. But the land of the Pharaohs does, after the neglect of centuries, because it is under trained English administration. I know a part of our own country so poor in natural resources that God must have forgotten to finish it; yet the people who live there make more kinds of useful and beautiful things than the same number of people make anywhere else in America and more of them are rich or well-to-do than the people in any other part of the country. And education engages as large a part of the population as any other single industry, and there is as much money spent on school-houses and their equipment and on libraries as is spent in the equipment of any single industry.

While natural resources count for much, the community where the people are trained to profitable industry is the community to which other men will go to live, and they will go from all parts of the world. After the first pioneer settlements are made, it is trained men that attract men rather than natural resources. The right training of men is a better thing than the bounty of Nature itself. Nature alone never made prosperous States.

But what commonplace things are these that I tire you with! They are only the A. B. C. of your philosophy and of your work. Yet if any should ask for proof of this doctrine, that it is the training of men that makes a country great, let him take a chapter out of the current history of the United States. The most remarkable spectacle that has ever been seen in the world is the spectacle of the trained American people at work to-day. From one ocean to the other they are so doing their daily labour that the products of their skill as well as the products of their soil are invading not only every new land, but every country of the Old World as well and the sleeping Orient to boot. In London the Englishman will soon go from his home to his office on an electric railway owned by Americans. He wears American shoes and uses American cutlery. If you cross Southern Europe on one of the fastest express trains, you will be drawn by an American locomotive. In Spain itself they use American engines and American machinery. And American locomotives whistle in African jungles and climb the Andes, and run across Japan. We have built bridges over rivers on the road to Mandalay. American electrical machinery lights the southernmost beacon on the globe in Terra del Fuego, and American machinery cuts timber at the northernmost lumber camps in Sweden, almost under the midnight sun, whither it was drawn on reindeer sleds. The lantern of Alladin has been superseded in Bagdad by American lamps. The coolies that fanned Indian princes have lost their job, for American electric fans do it better. We send laundry machinery to Shanghai, and brewing apparatus to Germany.

And it is not by mechanical work and mechanical achievements only that the trained American is covering the earth with his influence. We are bringing civilization and order to long neglected islands on both sides of the globe and proving that the true government of colonies is to teach them to govern themselves. We prevailed against the powers that prey in preventing the partition of China.

These achievements have a deeper meaning than the mere skill they show in diplomacy, in administration, in organization, in artisanship, and in trade, though the meaning of these is deep enough. They show that we have learned something in the training of men that no other people has learned, some method whereby every man may find his aptitude and may reach his most natural development. They show that we have found the secret of preserving the mobility of society whereby individuals may reach the highest efficiency with some certainty and not by chance.

The only advantage that Americans have over their kinsmen of the Old World is the advantage of free democratic training. We are no more capable by nature than the English, and we are not as well trained as the Germans, but we have greater social mobility, which is the very essence of democratic training. We have built a type of society that permits more men to find their natural places in it. And thus it is that the greatest contribution to social science, to the science of training men and of building States, is the demonstration that we have made of the ever-re-creative and ever-renewing quality of democratic society.

If the triumphs of trained democracy that are now filling the world with talk and wonder prove that the first duty of the State is the right training of all its children, see what this means for Georgia! There are more than two million pairs of hands and brains in Georgia. If they were all trained to wasteless work and to straight thought while they work, men would soon come from every land to learn of you. No other part of the globe would be so rich, no other part of the multitudinous swarms of mankind would be so blest. What would you have your Commonwealth become? The training place of the peaceful conquerors of the world? You have the material for making it so. The neglected boy of your sandhills might become, if he were rightly trained, a strong leader of men or a creator of great wealth. The tangle-haired girl that plays in your gulleys might become the mother of a greater statesman than you have yet bred. By training every one of them, but not by training some only, to a useful occupation and a steady balance of body and mind, in two generations, even before many of us here shall die, you may have more wealth, a better diffused well-being, a more robust manhood, greater grace, than Georgia in all her generations has yet had, and more renown than all the deeds of all her honourable sons have yet brought her.

Have you not merely played with education and missed the meaning of it, regarding it as an incident of juvenile life, or as a thing to confer a little distinction in conventional society? Have you kept it in mind that it is the science of building commonwealths? When you see its full meaning your State will grow under the patriotic ministrations of these its consecrated servants as well-tended gardens grow under the nurture of your Southern sun. And the Georgia of to-day, prosperous and fortunate as it is, is but a rew wilderness in comparison with the Georgia that may be.

Ladies and Gentlemen of this statecreative craft, the happiest of mortals have always been those who have worked under a great inspiration. Happiest of men and women are you, then, who have an inspiration that none has had since the fathers of our Republic. For you have dedicated yourselves to the most solemn high service of democracy; and the mute appeal of neglected children is to you the voice of God. It is your privilege to lead them who have been forgotten through the wide-swinging doors of opportunity; and thus you will develop the richest neglected resources of civilization. I feel honoured to applaud you as you go forth, not as workers for wages, but as rebuilders of this Commonwealth on a broader foundation than the fathers laid.

You whose privilege it is to labour here and we who have the pleasure to applaud you—let us together recite this creed:

I believe in the free public training of both the hands and the mind of every child born of woman.

I believe that by the right training of men we add to the wealth of the world. All wealth is the creation of man, and he creates it only in proportion to the trained uses of the community; and, the more men we train, the more wealth everyone may create.

I believe in the perpetual regeneration of society, in the immortality of democracy, and in growth everlasting.

We who have seen this truth have been changed by it! and we can never fall away from it. We have an inexhaustible supply of energy and a boundless hope. We work with joy for the love of our fellows and for our faith in them. We cannot rest for the glory of democracy as it has been revealed to us, for we are caught in the swing of its orbic movement. And we cannot recant even at the bidding of all the "solemn plausibilities of the world." We have learned the central secret of human progress. Since civilization began, religions and statecraft, priests and conquerors, cliques and classes, sects and sections of society have played for the leadership of man. We play for it, too; and we hold the master trick against them all; for, when we win, man leads himself.

The Rebuilding of Old Commonwealths

[*Reprinted from "The Atlantic Monthly," for May, 1902*]

I HAVE LATELY BEEN TO A NEIGHBOURHOOD IN ONE OF the Southern States that I knew twenty-five years ago. The railway station was then a flimsy shanty that the country merchant had himself built in payment for the railroad's stopping its one daily passenger train if it were signalled. It stopped twice or thrice a week and the passenger who got off or on felt himself a person with privileges. The one daily freight train stopped as seldom; and, when it stopped, it put off a box or a barrel for the merchant, but I think it never took anything on. Three families of importance lived near the railway station, and the little settlement dwindled down the muddy road to a dozen Negro shanties. All round about was a country population on small farms, and further away there were the wrecks of two old plantations.

In the neighbourhood were a Methodist church and a Baptist church. "Mother," said a pious Methodist girl of eighteen, "is it impossible for an Episcopalian to be saved?" For still the circuit-riding preacher at "revival" times insisted that the grace of God fell short of saving them that danced and played cards. The young people and occasionally a hoary sinner went to the mourners' bench and were duly "converted." Then the community rested from disturbing questions of faith till the Baptist "revival" came and the Elder insisted on the necessity of immersion.

There was a shanty down the road that was used for a school-house. A young woman taught a dozen children for $1 a month each till she was married. Then there was no school for two years. For a generation or two it had an intermittent life. A public school was kept for the very poor in a hut a mile away in the woods for about six weeks a year. Life ran easy and life ran slow. Politics and religion, each in its season, the crops and the promise of peaches, stories of fox-hunting and sometimes reminiscences of the war, were the staples of conversation.

Two railroads now run by the town and you may take a sleeping car on either one and go to New York in twenty hours, whereas twenty years ago it was a journey of fifty or sixty hours with several stops and there was no sleeping car. The town has mills and shops and paved streets and electric lights, a well-maintained private school and two public schools, one for whites and one for blacks. Society still divides itself into church-groups, but the violence of religious controversy is abated, especially among the men; for they now discuss the price of certain stocks in New York. Even whist parties are held at the home of a man of Baptist antecedents. The men have a wider range of activities and the women have more clothes. The spread of well-being has been general. The intellectual life has been quickened, although it yet shows some of its structural peculiarities. The people are becoming like village-folk wherever they have been touched but not radically changed by material prosperity. If the well-trained reader of *The Atlantic Monthly* who is looking for a problem were now to go to this town, she would go too late; for time is working its natural results in this American community and twenty years hence it will be (except for the presence of two races) very like hundreds of towns in the Middle West. It is true the people talk slowly and cut off their words; they read the worst newspapers in the world because they are "Democratic"; but, if they had better cooks, you would be content to live with them the rest of your life, for they give you good fellowship and they have the inestimable boon of leisure.

These good qualities of fellowship and leisure mark them off from the people of corresponding fortune and social gradation in most other parts of the country. They are not only demonstrative; they really care for one another in most affectionate ways. Helpfulness is not an act of conscience: it is an impulse. Hospitality is not a mere habit: it is a necessity of their natures. It was in a town like this that a plan was made to build a hotel; and, when the leading citizen was asked to subscribe to stock in the hotel-company, he replied with a touch of indignation: "A hotel? what do you want with a hotel? Whenever a gentleman comes to town I entertain him; and, if a man comes here who isn't a gentleman, let him go on." If you are a gentleman and go there, any man in the town will stop work for a day (or seem to stop it) to entertain you. His household and his business will seem to move wholly with reference to your comfort and convenience; and every man and woman you meet will be delighted to see you. They will tell you so and show you that they mean it. You will come away with the feeling that, though you had before known hospitable individuals and families, you now know a whole town that had nothing to do but to entertain you.

I can never forget or recall without a thrill of gratitude the distinction that was paid me several years ago when I went on an errand to a Southern city where I was almost a stranger. I had been at the hotel less than an hour when a gentleman whom I had not seen for twenty years called and took me to his home. His beautiful children did their share in entertaining me as if I had gone only to see them. I had a letter of introduction to a feeble old gentleman who lived nearly two miles away. I presented it and he seemed overwhelmed with regret that he could not return my call nor add to my entertainment. During my visit the venerable coloured servant of this fine old man rode to the house of my host every morning at eight o'clock and delivered this speech: "De Col'nel sent me to ax consarnin' Mr. Page's helf. He hopes he slep' well an' feels refreshed dis mawnin' and he 'spesses de hope dat you is all well." God rest his soul! he opposed most ideas that I think sound, but he loved all men and women that are lovely and strong; and he was a radiant gentleman.

If you are determined to find a problem, you may reflect on this—how in the march of industrialism these qualities of fellowship and leisure may be retained in the mass of the people; and how they might be transplanted to corresponding towns in other parts of the Union? It is not a trick, not a mere fashion or a tradition: it is a quality of the blood—a touch of nature that would redeem the unlovely wastes of much more prosperous and better-informed life.

A few months ago I rode for more than a hundred miles along this first railway that ran by the village that I have described, in the company of a man who has gradually amassed a fortune by the good management of a cotton-mill. As we passed a dozen such towns he said that he had always believed in the success of "our people." They are as capable as any people under the sun and are better neighbours than most," said he. "But I had no idea that I should ever live to see such a degree of financial prosperity as they have already reached." Then after a long talk about the growth of these communities he remarked—"Schools, schools, schools of the right sort—that is what we need."

But in the country about these towns men and women are essentially like the men and women who lived there fifty years ago, or eighty years, or even a hundred. The farmers have more money than their predecessors had, but the general structure of their life is the same—a dull succession of the seasons where agriculture is practised in old-fashioned ways, where weary housewives show resignation rather than contentment and where ignorance has become satisfied with itself. The country is somewhat more densely populated than it was twenty years ago but the growth of population suggests only a denser stagnation.

These men and women do not feel poor. They have a civilization of their own, of which they are very proud. They have for a hundred years been told to be proud of it. The politicians have told them that they are the best people on earth, that the State they live in is the most important in the Union, that the ideas they stand for are the bulwarks of our liberties. Do they not own land? Are they not independent? What more could men ask? One in five is illiterate. But what matter? Some of the illiterate men are more successful than some others that can read. What does it profit a man, then, to read? There is a self-satisfied personal dignity which these men show that prevents near approach. If you propose to change any law or custom, or are suspected of such a wish, or if you come with a new idea, the burden of proving its value is on you. What they are they regard as the normal state of human society. There was talk in one neighbourhood, I recall, about the possibility that the son of one of the more prosperous of these men might go away to study medicine. "I don't see the use," said the father. "We've got two doctors nigh enough and there ain't no room for a third." The preacher, too, has hardened their self-contentment, especially the self-contentment of the women, by fixing their attention on the life to come, almost to the exclusion of ambition to lift up the life that is.

A country schoolmaster in this region told me last year (truly enough) that the ability to read was not a good test even of a man's intelligence, to say nothing of his character. "Why, do you know," asked he, "how many of the Confederate soldiers were illiterate? And they were the best soldiers that ever went to war."

"Suppose they had all been trained—trained to some useful occupation, some as geologists, some as miners, some as machinists, some as shipwrights, some as gun-makers; the iron in Alabama, the wood and coal near by —would these not have been utilized in war?"

"Utilized? We'd 've whipped the Yankees—shore!"

"What would you think of schools where men should now be trained to occupations—schools here in this neighbourhood, to make ploughs, waggons, furniture— everything?"

"That'd be a mighty good thing; but that ain't education."

There is, of course, a considerable variety of social conditions here as everywhere else in the world. Near one home where both children and grandchildren are illegitimate is the residence of a man who holds his land by direct descent in his family from a colonial grant, and whose sons are successful lawyers and preachers in four States. A good many youth go to the towns and find wider opportunities. From this same neighbourhood a young man went to New York and is a rich merchant there; another went to college by his own exertions and is an electrical engineer in a great manufacturing city; another is a partner in a factory in New England; another is a judge in Oregon. The most ambitious of course, go away; and the general level of life seems to remain as low as it was generations ago. The number of emigrants from the old Southern States tells the story of the stagnation of life in these rural regions.

Three influences have held the social structure stationary—first, slavery, which pickled all Southern life and left it just as it found it; then the politician and the preacher. One has proclaimed the present as the ideal condition; and, if any doubt this declaration, the other has bidden him be content and make sure of the world to come. Thus gagged and bound this rural society has remained stationary longer than English-speaking people have remained stationary anywhere else in the world. It is a state of life that keeps permanently the qualities of the frontier civilization long after the frontier has receded and been forgotten. The feeling that you bring away with you after a visit to such a community is a feeling that something has intervened to hold these people back from their natural development. They have capacity that far outruns their achievement. They are citizens of an earlier time and of a narrower world who have not come to their own. And this is the cue to their character.

The familiar classification of the Southern people as "gentlemen" and "poor whites" is misleading. The number of the large landed proprietors and of large slaveholders has been greatly exaggerated by tradition. Smaller, too, than is thought is the class that may properly be called "white trash" or "buckra." The great mass of these people came of sturdy English and Scotch-Irish stock and they are very like the country population that settled the other States eighty years or more ago. They are not poorer nor "trashier" than the rural population of New Jersey or Pennsylvania or New York or New England were several generations ago, nor than they are now in some remote regions of these States.

If the rural parts of New York or New Jersey or of Pennsylvania were to-day depopulated and all the machinery of the present civilization were removed, and if to-morrow the population of eighty years ago were to reappear just as it was, this would be a community very like these Southern communities. What an interesting field for sociological experiment such a reappearance of a part of the past would present! Peddlers, missionaries, and reorganizers of social life would overwhelm their "contemporary ancestors." It would be a pleasure to help them forward in a decade as far as their descendants travelled in eighty years, but it would not be an easy task. After many impatient efforts we should learn the wisdom of trying to find out their point of view and of contenting ourselves with seeing them advance in their own way, even if they came slowly and seemed stupid. Teaching one's ancestors is at best a difficult undertaking; for it is not the same task as teaching one's descendants. What a lot of disappointing effort this generation might have saved if it had known this simple truth somewhat sooner!

I have purposely not written of the Negro as a separate part of the population, for in the building up of the commonwealth he will yield to the same kind of training. The Negro, at once the beneficiary and the victim of slavery, yet holds the white man, who was its victim and not its beneficiary, in economic bondage; and he is himself also in economic bondage and in bondage likewise to the white man's race-feeling. Training that brings economic independence sets the strongest and most natural forces of life at play. I long doubted whether a democracy could absorb two different races thus living together and yet apart. But the practical results of right training, both on the white man and on the Negro, have left no room for doubt, I think, in the mind of any far-seeing man who has made a personal study of these results. The doubtful thing is whether within any calculable time they will all receive right training.

Without right training, you have such a problem as men nowhere else in our country have. It will yield little to reason. Argument will not solve it. Time alone will bring slow change. The preacher cannot help; for the races have fallen apart in their religious life. The politicians have only made the race-relations worse. The white man has held the Negro back, the Negro has held the white man back; and dead men have ruled them both. Training to economic independence is the only true emancipation.

Distinctive Southern life is to be found not only in the country but in certain old towns also. A college-town will serve as an example. I know such a community where it seems proper to rest till one die, so quiet is its mild, contented life, so dignified the houses and the trees, and so peaceful the half-neglected gardens. You are aware only of an invitation to repose. When a route for a railroad half a century or more ago was run through a college-town very like this there was great excitement. A railroad? Never! It would jar the dignity of the community and corrupt the morals of youth. It was deflected, therefore; and, after thirty years of jolting in hacks over bad roads, the people had to build a branch railroad. But even then they would not permit a locomotive nearer than a mile. The railroad, therefore, ended in an old field and the same hacks yet have their share of work to do. But the old field is now the site of a cotton mill.

I recently visited a college-town contemporary with this. The century-old buildings, the elms and the oaks that give acres of shade—trees some of which were planted by great men with proper ceremonies—in such an atmosphere generation after generation of youth has absorbed a little learning and much patriotism. The young men you meet are grave in manner, earnest fellows who have already dedicated themselves to the State; for the State is greater than the Nation.

It was in this academic circle more than a decade ago that I asked a member of the faculty why he attended a particular church, for I knew that he had for many years been an "adherent" of another sect and a believer in none. "I throw beef to the lion," said he. "The sectarian representation in this faculty must be evenly balanced, and by this adjustment I belong to the church that I attend." He unlocked a door in his library and took out a handful of books, Matthew Arnold's "Literature and Dogma," a volume of Renan and two or three others. "These I keep under lock and key."

It was in this college town that I went to rest last winter. My memory will suffer palsy before I forget the unchanging charm of that academic circle of eighteenth-century life; for it is as it was before anything was that now is in our country. The succession of generations is an incident; the coming of men from other States and other lands—it is they that soon change, not this circle into which they come. Tradition is king here and there is no other. You would wear his livery yourself within an hour after you entered his kingdom; and you feel at home, as you would feel at home if you could visit your ancestors from whom you were reprehensible for straying away into your own generation.

When the play of general conversation had ended one evening the talk settled down to a specific topic, and this was the topic—the lack of freedom of speech in the community. Of course, there was in that company absolute freedom. We were talking about "radical" opinions, especially on theological subjects and about the race-relation. "I should not dare," said one Professor, "to say in public—in my lecture-room or in print—a single thing that I have said here."

"Why?"

"I should be dismissed."

"Do the men who hold the power of dismissal *all* count your opinions a crime?"

"Why, not one of them. They all agree with me. There is no difference of private opinion. I can discuss anything with them in private. But they could not withstand the public indignation that would be expressed through the press."

"This is the more remarkable," another added with a laugh, "because the editor of the most important newspaper in this quarter of the world holds more 'radical' opinions than any other man I know. But he has to serve the public."

"Who is the public?"

"The Democratic platform, the Daughters of the Confederacy, old General So-and-so, and the Presbyterian creed," said one.

"And the farmers who vote whether they can read or not," added another.

As for the editor of the powerful newspaper, I knew that a year before he had sought an engagement in New York, in order "to get out of the realm that is ruled by the dead."

It is in such a circle of the old academic society and in rural regions that you come upon the real Southern problem—that unyielding stability of opinion which gives a feeling of despair, the very antithesis of social growth and of social mobility. "Everything lies here where it fell," said a village philosopher in speaking of this temper. "There are the same rocks in the road that were there before the war."

To illustrate—one morning I went to a school for the Negroes and I heard a very black boy translate and construe a passage of Xenophon. His teacher also was a full-blooded Negro. It happened that I went straight from the school to a club where I encountered a group of gentlemen discussing the limitations of the African mind.

"Teach 'em Greek!" said old Judge So-and-so. "Now a nigger could learn the Greek alphabet by rote, but he could never intelligently construe a passage from any Greek writer—impossible!" I told him what I had just heard. "Read it? Understand it? was black? a black man teaching him? I beg your pardon, but do you read Greek yourself?"

"Sir," said he at last, "I do not for a moment doubt your word. I know you think the nigger read Greek; but you were deceived. I shouldn't believe it if I saw it with my own eyes and heard it with my own ears."

Such are the baffling facts of a sparse population and of a self-satisfied life that lingers past its day. Do they give reason for despair? Not at all; but they do give reason for patience. The problem is the most important that has been presented in our national life. It is not the education of a few millions of neglected persons; it is not the modernizing of a few picturesque institutions; least of all is it the task of imposing on these people the civilization that has been developed elsewhere (for this would be a fool's errand indeed and in no way desirable if it were possible); but the larger question is this:—

Since democracy means constant social growth and social mobility, is Southern life becoming democratic or is it remaining stable, or going back to an essentially aristocratic structure? Are forces inside it asserting themselves that give promise of shaping this life in line with democratic growth? Or are the native forces reactionary? Is democracy there at last to be a failure? Is it equal to the task of assimilating the master race and the freed race?

There are thoughtful men who frankly deny the possibility of such a complete conquest by the democratic idea. I quote one such, a man of learning if not of wisdom, who wrote this memorandum for me under the mistletoe in an old South Carolina mansion last winter:

"The dominant elements of society in the two sections of the country were different from the beginning. Slavery did not make the difference, it only emphasized it. The unconscious aims and ideals of the two peoples diverged. The abolition of slavery was a matter of force. So also was the suppression of secession. But these events did not change the essential character of the people. Superficially they are now one. But forty years are as nothing in the life of a people, nor fifty years nor a hundred. The South is to-day further from a willing acceptance of real democratic ideals than it was twenty years ago. The growth of such organizations as the Daughters of the Confederacy, the increasing celebration of the heroism of the Confederate soldier, the silent unwillingness of white men to tax themselves to educate the Negro, the instinctive denial to the Negro of any real standing in the most important matters of life—these things seem to me to point to a different genius, a different tendency, a different ideal, even a different necessity. How the divergence will work itself out, I do not know, but a century hence the South will be, in the essence of its civilization, further from the North than it now is. No outward forms of government can make two different peoples the same."

Another man of learning if not of wisdom used to say to me in Cambridge, Massachusetts: "The Southerners have always seemed foreigners to me. The Northern and the Southern people are different. I do not think they will ever work out the same ideals."

These opinions (which I have heard in recent years only in South Carolina and in Massachusetts and only in academic circles) strip the question of all side issues and of all temporary aspects. It is true that the same laws may not mean the same thing North and South (as the XIVth amendment to the Federal Constitution does not); and forty years have not essentially changed the Negro's place in the community; and it is true that no exterior or temporary influence counts for much and the hereditary "essence of a civilization" is everything. No man of thought has ever regarded laws enacted at Washington against the consent of the Southern people as a primary force in shaping their life, nor outside aid to education or to anything else as revolutionary if it

ran counter to the native "genius"; preaching is of no
avail; alms-giving is an estranging force; in a word, if
Southern life have not in it the seed and the necessity
of a true democratic development, then a democratic
order cannot be thrust upon it and it were useless to try.

But, if I understand the great forces of our time, and
if I know the history of the people of the Southern commonwealths (which to the obscuring of the whole large
matter remains unwritten), my friends from whom I
have quoted have made a radical misinterpretation of
all the large facts and of all dominant present tendencies.
There is no undemocratic trait in the Southern people
that is not directly accounted for by slavery and by the
results of slavery. The most conspicuous institutional
results were the political machines that were built on
race differences first by one political party and then by
the other, and the ecclesiastical machines that are the
direct result of popular ignorance and isolation. The
country people that I have described are men of good
mettle, men to make free commonwealths of. The very
strongest impulse they have is patriotic and democratic.
The contrary tendencies are clearly survivals of a deflec-
tion of their development. So strongly have I been im-
pressed with the democratic quality of Southern character that I believe, if a democracy existed nowhere in

the world, Southern life would now evolve one, perhaps even of a radical type.

These old commonwealths were arrested in their development by slavery and by war and by the double burden of a sparse population and of an ignorant alien race. When the weight of these burdens is considered, the progress made these thirty years in the development of the innate democratic tendency is without parallel in our history. The present backwardness of Southern life in rural communities and in old academic or social circles is but a picturesque reminder of the distance we have travelled. Descriptions of these may entertain us, as the charm of the obsolete appeals to all cultivated minds, but they give no hint except by contrast of the real forces of the period in which we live.

The process that has been going on in the upland South in particular is a process of conscious and natural State-building, constructive at every important step. Reactionary influences have been respectable, but they are spent impulses. There are two great constructive forces. The first is Industry, which has already given the essential power over to a class of men that bring mobility to social life and opportunity to them that can take it. This industrial development would finally work out the inherent democratic tendency of the people if no other force were brought into play. But no man who knows the gentleness and the dignity and the leisure of the old Southern life would like to see these qualities blunted by too rude a growth of sheer industrialism.

The other great force that frankly recognizes the arrested development of the people and is taking hold of the problem of their natural growth is the new impulse in public education. This is native, and it is nothing different from Jefferson's creed and plan. So strong is it that its recent manifestation may fairly be called a new chapter in our national history. In the presence of this revolutionary force, fear of reaction and doubt about the democratic "essence" of Southern civilization falls away. Beside this all other forces except the force of industrial life count for nothing.

Formal education has been going on in the South these thirty years with increasing efficiency in the cities and the large towns and at the colleges. There are communities in which the whole attitude towards modern life has been changed by the influence of the schools. But it is not of town life, nor of higher education, that I now write. I write rather of that new impulse for the right training of the neglected masses that is a larger matter than school-room work or academic or professional training—of the subject as it affects the direction of the whole people's development. From this point of view a dozen or two colleges count for little, however excellent they may be; and life in the cities is, in a sense, of secondary importance, because the cities are few and the wide stretches of rural life are almost immeasurable.

The situation is discouraging enough, Heaven knows. In the ten cis-Mississippian Southern States the proportion of illiterate white voters is as large as it was in 1850; and the public schools in these States now give "five cents' worth of education per child per day for only eighty-seven days a year." This is to say that the total expenditure on the public schools is five cents a schoolday per pupil and they are kept open an average of only eighty-seven days a year. But it is precisely because the situation is so bad that it is becoming so hopeful. Schools of this sort are little better than none. The people do not care for them. The stolidity of ignorance can not be overcome by any such perfunctory attack as this. The leaders of the best Southern opinion have come to recognize this truth, and they have begun work in a new way. They have discovered that the schools must do something more than teach the three R's, for a people without diversified occupations and without training do not care for the three R's, nor do the three R's profit them greatly. An idle and unproductive man is no less useless because he can read and write.

It was this fundamental fact that General Armstrong saw when he worked out the system of training towards occupations at Hampton Institute for the Negroes; and it is this fundamental fact that the present leaders of popular education in the Southern States understand. They are training hand and mind together. The experience in every rural community where a school of this kind has been established is that the people who cared nothing for what they called "education" are so eager for this training that they will make any sacrifice to obtain it. Herein is the beginning of a complete change in neglected village and rural life. Here, too, is proof that the people are not "in the essence of their civilization" different from the people of the other parts of the country. The "way out" has been found. The problem that the South now presents has at last become so plain that thoughtful men no longer differ about it. It is no longer obscured by race differences, nor by political differences. It is simply the training of the untrained masses. As slavery and war and an isolated life arrested their development and held them in a fixed social condition, so the proper training of them to helpful occupations will release them to usefulness in a democracy.

The new movement is revolutionary for another reason. The old notion of education was that it meant the training of a few. It is now understood that none can be well educated unless all are trained. The failure to educate the masses has sometimes brought tragic results to the educated. There was a man, for instance, in an old Southern town who became a famous scholar in the law; and I suppose that he was a man of very unusual learning. He became a judge, and he was regarded as the foremost jurist in his State. But his income hardly kept his library replenished. He lived in respectable want and died without making provision for his family. His son also was trained to the law; and, since the family felt it a sort of sacred duty that he should remain where he was born, his practice, too, was so small that he became discouraged and his life was a failure. The daughter sold the family mansion to pay the family debts. "But," as one of her neighbours said, "she is the first happy and independent member of that family." She teaches wood-work in the public school, and is training her nephews to scientific agriculture.

The men and women of both races who are leading this great popular movement work with an inspiration that puts conventional teachers to shame. For example: A young agricultural chemist several years ago began with enthusiasm a campaign of education among the farmers. He put much faith in bulletins and leaflets, which were sent broadcast. "I soon found out," said he, "that sending out literature did little good as long as many farmers could not read, and many more would not." He left his laboratory and became an educational statesman, and there are few men in America whose influence in building up the people is greater than his. Out of a comparatively small acquaintance, I know many similar experiences. A well-trained preacher for example, who has had much to do with the administration of the churches of his sect in rural regions lately gave up his work and became a superintendent of public schools. "Till the country people are educated," said he, "church work will not stick."

Any one who knows the work that such men are doing could fill these pages with a bare catalogue of heroic deeds—deeds like these for example: The principal of a school for training white teachers proposed to the faculty that they give a part of their salaries, which were meagre to the edge of poverty, to erect a new building for the school. Not one demurred. The building was put up, but there is yet not room enough for the self-supporting students that apply for admission; and twelve teachers have only four recitation rooms. They are occupied almost every hour of the day. Yet no sooner had their winter vacation come than the principal hurried to Hampton Institute to study its method of teaching handicrafts; and half the faculty went to New York to hear lectures at the Teachers' College. A vacation does not suggest rest to them but opportunity to equip themselves better. One of them went, as soon as his vacation began, to organize a model school in a village of two hundred people. They had collected $1,000. He secured $500 from some other source. The building was opened and every white parent in the neighbourhood went to the dedication of it; and the school, with its garden, its kitchen and its workshop as well as its books, provokes such enthusiasm as the community never would have felt for a mere book-school.

Educational work in these States is, therefore, something more than the teaching of youth; it is the building of a new social order. The far-reaching quality of the work that the energetic educators in the South are doing lifts them out of the ranks of mere schoolmasters and puts them on the level of constructive statesmen. They are the servants of democracy in a sense that no other public servants now are; for they are the re-builders of these old commonwealths.

Any man who has the privilege to contribute even so small a thing as applause to this great movement feels the thrill of this State-building work so strongly that he is not likely to take a keen interest in such tame exercise as historical speculation. Yet it would be interesting to speculate on the effects of Jefferson's plan for public education if it had been carried out. Would the public schools not have prevented the growth of slavery? True, public schools and slavery, as well as most other human institutions, are the results of economic forces; but, if the masses of the Southern population had been educated, or trained to work (and such training is education), a stronger economic impetus might have been given to diversified pursuits than cotton-culture gave to slavery, and the whole course of our history might have been changed. But, whatever may have been the results of Jefferson's educational policy if it had been worked out in Virginia, the development of Southern life in the next hundred years will be determined by the success with which it shall now be worked out. The nature of the problem is clear. The work will be slow and the recovery from these last effects of slavery may require as long a time as it required to abolish slavery; but of the ultimate result no man who can distinguish dominant from incidental forces can have a doubt.

The Southern people were deflected from their natural development. They are the purest American stock we have. They are naturally as capable as any part of our population. They are now slowly but surely working out their own destiny; and that destiny is a democratic order of society which will be an important contribution to the Republic that their ancestors took so large a part in establishing. Rich undeveloped resources of American life lie in these great rural stretches that are yet almost unknown. The foremost patriotic duty of our time is to hasten their development.

Set in Linotype Fairfield
Format by David Rosenberg
Manufactured by The Haddon Craftsmen, Inc.
Published by HARPER & BROTHERS, New York